GOOD VIBRATIONS

The Complete Guide to Vibrators

GOOD VIBRATIONS

The Complete Guide to Vibrators

Joani Blank

Preface by Betty Dodson
Illustrations by Marcia Quackenbush

Being a Treatise on the Use of Machines in the Indolent Indulgence of Erotic Pleasure-seeking, Together with Important Hints on the Acquisition, Care and Utilization of Said Machines, and Much More about the Art and Science of Buzzing Off.

Down There Press

San Francisco, California

Library of Congress Cataloging-in-Publication Data

```
Blank, Joani, 1937-
    Good Vibrations : the complete guide to vibrators :
  being a treatise on the use of machines in the indolent
  indulgence of erotic pleasure-seeking, together with im-
  portant hints on the acquisition, care, and utilization
  of said machines, and much more about the art and
  science of buzzing off / Joani Blank : illustrations by
  Marcia Quackenbush.
        p.    cm.
    Bibliography: p.
    ISBN 0-940208-12-1 : $5.50
    1. Masturbation. 2. Vibrators. 3. Female orgasm.
  I. Title.
  HQ447.B54 1989
  613.9'6—dc20                             89-34171
```

We also offer librarians an Alternative CIP prepared by Sanford Berman, Head Cataloger at Hennepin County Library, Edina, Minnesota, which we believe more fully reflects this book's scope and content.

Alternative Cataloging-in-Publication Data

```
Blank, Joani.
    Good vibrations: the complete guide to vibrators.
  Illustrations by Marcia Quackenbush. Revised and expanded
  ed. Burlingame, CA: Down There Press, copyright 1989.
    PARTIAL CONTENTS: History. -Oddities. Eggs. Ben-Wa balls.
  -Buying a vibrator. -User's manual. Doing what feels
  good. Care and feeding of your vibrator. -Women and
  vibrators. -Men and vibrators. -Vibrators and your
  partner. -Health considerations and special uses.
    1. Vibrators. 2. Sex manuals. 3. Masturbation. 4.Women-
  Sexuality. 5. Men-Sexuality. 6. Ben-Wa balls. I. Title.
  II. Title: The complete guide to vibrators. III. Down
  There Press. IV. Quackenbush, Marcia, illus.
```

Cover Illustration: Betty Dodson (adapted by Mariane Zenker)
Cover Design: Mariane Zenker
Project Manager: Leigh Dickerson Davidson

Additional copies of *Good Vibrations* are available at your local bookstore or directly from the publisher:

Down There Press, 938 Howard Street, San Francisco CA 94103
Please enclose $8.75 for each copy ordered, which includes UPS shipment and handling. California residents please add sales tax.

Printed in the United States of America   9 8 7 6 5

Table of Contents

Also by Joani Blank

A Kid's First Book About Sex

The Playbook for Kids About Sex

The Playbook for Men About Sex

The Playbook for Women About Sex

Herotica 2 (co-editor, with Susie Bright, NAL/Plume)

Femalia (editor)

Foreword to the Third Edition

AFTER TWENTY-THREE YEARS of using an electric vibrator, I am still discovering new experiences with pleasure and orgasm. In the beginning I admit I was a bit worried about walking off into the sunset with my electric friend in hand, never to be heard from again. But since I have continued to also enjoy "people sex," I have finally stopped worrying about becoming vibrator addicted. I've neither worn my clitoris down to a nub nor become antisocial.

As a sex teacher I have taught the use of the electric vibrator for selfloving to thousands of women who have taken my Bodysex workshops, or who have read my book *Sex For One: The Joy of SelfLoving*. For the pre-orgasmic woman, an electric vibrator is heaven sent. This strong, consistent and reliable form of stimulation can reestablish the connection of the nerve pathways from the clitoris to the brain. Women in their thirties, forties, fifties and beyond can discover erotic feelings after a lifetime of sexual repression, sexual deprivation or lack of sexual interest. Sexual energy is healing.

Some women say they don't need a vibrator because they have a loving partner who gives them all the orgasms they want. There is no rule that says a woman must use a vibrator to be fully sexual. But over time, monogamy and marriage tend toward boredom, and that's when vibrators and other sex toys can be introduced for sexual variety. Whether it comes from a lover, a finger, a dildo or a vibrator, an orgasm is an orgasm is an orgasm.

Orgasms come in many colors, textures, sizes and forms of pleasure. For me there is no such thing as a "bad" orgasm. I love the happy little orgasms I get from a fifteen minute sex-break. At the other end of my scale are the intense orgasms that are part of a two-hour selfloving ritual with my electric vibrator and a dildo. It's a cosmic flight of joy — breathing, rocking, riding the waves of ecstacy. My electric orgasms put me in touch with my sexual and spiritual power as I become one with the goddess of love.

Joani Blank has been a pioneering sex counselor and educator, breaking ground in the field of female sexuality with her own books, her vibrator store and her publishing company. Our ongoing exchange of information has enriched both of our efforts to better understand our own, and other women's, sexuality. Joani has enhanced the erotic lives of millions of women and their partners.

First published in 1977, *Good Vibrations* is a classic in its field. It has a wealth of information about sexuality and orgasm as well as vibrators. Since electric orgasms are still relatively unknown, this book is a must for women and men who want to explore sexual pleasure in depth.

Betty Dodson
Summer, 1989

Author's note: Betty says very little about men in this preface, but I know for certain that she thinks all this stuff applies to them too. *J.B.*

Once Upon A Time...

I WALKED A FEW TIMES past the department store salesclerk who was eagerly demonstrating the big blue and white massager. "On sale — only $19.50 today," she said. Although I had heard about sexual uses for electric vibrators, I couldn't justify spending twenty dollars just to try the massager for masturbation. So I turned my back and asked her to hold the whirring machine to a chronically tight spot on my right shoulder. The massager was stronger than any I'd ever felt. The low speed produced a deep throbbing sensation. The high speed was so fast it either tickled or hurt, depending on how it was touching me. It hurt my shoulder so good

> *"In Redbook's sex survey, of 100,000 women, one out of five said they used some 'device' during their lovemaking, and for more than half of those women that device was a vibrator."* [16]

that I bought it without further hesitation. At the time, and for some weeks later, I didn't even try masturbating with it.

Up until then, the only way I had masturbated was with my hand, occasionally using an object in my vagina at the same time. I had inserted the handle of my electric toothbrush into my vagina, enjoying the gentle vibrations and warmth, but it had not occurred to me to use it on or near my clitoris. Within moments after I held the new blue and white vibrator to my clitoris, I experienced the most intense orgasm of my life. Although it was all over before I knew what was happening, I saw great potential for pleasure in my new toy.

My partner and I, being yard sale and flea market fanatics, started to collect "antique" and just plain old vibrators and massagers at every opportunity. After a couple of years, we had acquired more than thirty treasures. At first, I tried masturbating with every one and found, to my delight, that all of them, regardless of size, shape, or intensity of vibration, gave me orgasms. We kept them amid the jumble of their own cords and loose attachments in a fabric suitcase under our bed. Periodically we would haul out the suitcase, untangle a few, and plug them in for our friends to giggle or marvel at. Some went out on loan and never returned.

During this time, I was being trained as a sex therapist and was working with many

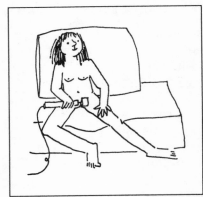

women who had never experienced orgasm. The women in my groups who wanted to experiment with vibrators expressed distress about how awkward they felt purchasing them. Shortly thereafter, I decided to open Good Vibrations, a vibrator store especially (though certainly not exclusively) for women, with a vibrator museum (actually an antique oak showcase) for the public display of our collection. I also wrote and published the first version of this book.

Since 1975, I have learned a great deal about vibrators. In the store, I have had the opportunity to talk with hundreds of women and dozens of men about all aspects of vibrator use. During this time, people have talked more and more openly about vibrators. Sales of vibrators in drug, department and discount stores have mushroomed. In these settings, of course, advertising and promotion are still aimed at the consumers' sore muscles and tired feet. However, once many of these vibrators get home and out of the box, they probably spend most of their turned-on moments turning someone on. People are not only using vibrators more, they are also increasingly talking, writing and reading about them.

The "Hysterical" History of the Vibrator

DID YOU EVER WONDER what mysterious ailment confined the Victorian woman to her bed? Our prim and proper ancestor had the doctor scurrying up the stairs with his little black bag and the servants whispering about "female troubles."

Not infrequently, those "female troubles" were "hysteria," believed in ancient Egypt and Greece to be the revolt of the uterus against sexual deprivation. Webster's reminds us that "hysteria" derives from "the former notion that hysteric women were suffering from disturbances of  the womb" (now you know why men are almost never hysterical!) and defines it as a "psychoneurosis marked by emotional excitability and disturbances of the psychic, sensory, vasomotor and visceral functions." It wasn't until 1952 that the American Psychiatric Association dismissed hysteria as a valid diagnosis.

3

Historian Rachel Maines has recently provided us with a wealth of information about the standard medical treatment of "hysteria" using vibrators.[12, 13] Maines shows that "the electromechanical vibrator, introduced as a medical appliance in the 1880s and as a household appliance between 1900 and 1905, represented a de-skilling and capital-labor substitution innovation designed to improve the efficiency of medical massage, a task performed since ancient times by physicians, midwives and their assistants." Medical massage "from the time of Hippocrates to that of Freud included the clinical production of orgasm in women and girls."

According to medical and midwifery texts of the 1600s, "the treatment generally consisted of the insertion of one or more fingers of one hand into the vagina and the application of friction to the external genitalia with the other. Fragrant oils of various types were employed as lubricants in this procedure." The objective was to induce "hysterical paroxysm," manifested by "rapid respiration and pulse, reddening of the skin, vaginal lubrication and abdominal contractions." Sounds very familiar, doesn't it, but at the time it was considered an activity more appropriate to the doctor's office than the boudoir!

Maines writes that not all physicians recognized this "paroxysm" as an orgasm, but some medical authors through the ages do "comment on the morally ambiguous character of the treatment, including [one physician] who observes that genital massage should be reserved 'to those alone who have clean hands and a pure heart'." Later therapies included massage with a jet of water, but "hydrotherapists warned that patients were inclined to demand more treatment than was considered good for them." A seventeenth century doctor complained of the fatigue factor for the physician in massage therapy and the long practice and considerable dexterity required (not to mention the stress of keeping those hands clean and those hearts pure).

Maines credits George Taylor, an American physician, with a primary role in the development of the modern vibrator in this country. In 1869 and 1872 he patented a steam-powered massage and vibratory apparatus for treatment of female disorders, intended for supervised use "to prevent overindulgence." By 1900, "a wide range of vibratory apparatus was available to physicians....Articles and textbooks on vibratory massage technique at the turn of the century praised the machines' versatility for treatment of nearly all diseases in both sexes, and its [sic] efficiency of time and labor, especially in gynecological massage....By [1909] convenient portable models were available, permitting use on house calls...." (So that's what was inside the doctor's little black bag.)

Until the end of the 1920s, vibrators were advertised in respectable women's

> *"Has achieving orgasm become just another way of releasing the tensions of day-to-day living? Has the vibrator, once considered a therapeutic device, become a sort of microwave oven of the bedroom — a fast, efficient means of getting sexual pleasure? Is the most efficient orgasm the best orgasm? Is the bedroom really the place for a time-saving device? If so, what are we saving all this time for?"* [18]

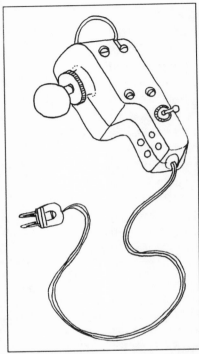

magazines as home appliances, primarily as an aid to good health and relaxation, but with ambiguous overtones — "All the pleasures of youth will throb within you," reads a typical ad. Maines believes that the disappearance of vibrators from doctors' offices and magazine advertisements "may have been the result either of the adoption of psychotherapeutic treatments [for hysteria] by physicians, or of the appearance of vibrators in stag films in the Twenties, or both."

Most of the electric vibrators discussed in this book were neither designed nor marketed (until very recently) with sexual uses in mind.

In a 1981 *Esquire* article,[18] author Mimi Swartz reviewed the emergence of the vibrator as a big business venture, with sales totaling about $13 million in 1980. This is a remarkable story when you consider that the manufacturers are marketing a product without advertising its main benefit. Imagine trying to sell a toaster by saying that it is a metal box that gets very hot when you plug it in — and that's all. Apparently, this non-existent marketing approach failed, since several mainstream manufacturers no longer make vibrators.

Electric vibrators/massagers have been manufactured in the United States since around the turn of the century (the most elderly in my collection was made by Hamilton Beach and carries a patent date of 1902). However, the first electric vibrator openly advertised for sexual use was an American-made, multi-attachment model, repackaged with a clitoral stimulator tip, and sold at first almost exclusively through the mail in the early 1970s. This particular brand is now sold primarily by discount stores alongside the hair dryers and electric toothbrushes. The package insert is pretty tame; all sexual references have disappeared. In the late 1980s, a well-stocked department or discount store in some parts of the country may carry as many as four or five different brands of electric vibrators, and lest rural readers despair, the Sears catalog has always included a full line of good quality vibrators (manufactured for them by others). Are you surprised?

Interesting, isn't it, that vibrators which lost their respectability once they were shunned by the medical profession are now seen as an important tool for women taking control of and enhancing their sexuality.

Old Vibrators

Most of the old, second-hand, used or antique vibrators you find at thrift stores, flea markets and garage sales are electric, not battery-operated. Some of the oldest are huge and heavy, while others are amazingly compact. If the case is not cracked or the motor inside is not loose, they are often very quiet. One

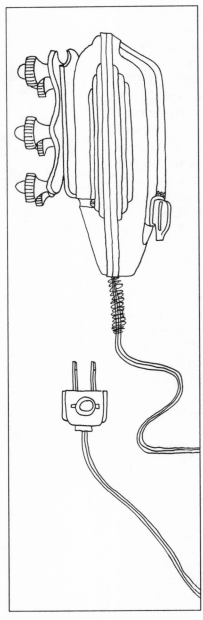

oldie we have, with a metal case and screw-on attachments, is so quiet that you can't tell whether it's on unless you are holding it. Old vibrators come in all shapes and sizes. We have one which closely resembles an old electric drill without the drill bit; another has six little, plastic vibrating "feet" and looks like a cross between a 1950s automobile and a miniature submarine. Although it's about thirty years old it has four "speeds."

Most older, multi-speed vibrators change intensity with a mechanism that tightens and loosens the vibrating head. The motor itself does not run faster and slower. Some of the very old machines don't have an on-off switch; it's on and you're off! As to cost, ours have ranged from 50¢ to $10.00. Others sell for as much as $25.00-$30.00. If you are going to buy a used vibrator for anything other than a good laugh, plug it in to be sure it works before you hand over your money. Usually they are not worth repairing. Of course, if the cord is frayed or if anything is obviously loose inside, you may not even want to plug it in for fear of an electric shock.

So Many To Choose From

IN GENERAL, ELECTRIC VIBRATORS are strong, quiet and well-made by brand name electrical appliance companies that do not acknowledge the sexual pleasure potential of their products. An electric vibrator will last for years, it will not electrocute you — as long as you keep it out of water — and it is well worth the investment and trouble of an extension cord if your bedroom outlet isn't handy.

Battery-operated vibrators, on the other hand, usually are advertised for sexual purposes. Among the advantages of these vibrators are their portability and wide variety of sizes and styles. Their drawbacks include their loudness, generally shoddy quality, and short lifetime.

Some companies that manufacture multiple-attachment massagers have tacitly acknowledged that at least some of their customers might use their products for sex, by including among the attachments one for "those special, hard-to-reach spots." Of course, the promotional materials, boxes, and package inserts say nothing about sex. In fact, some mainstream manufacturers of personal care products publicly deny the sexual uses of their wares, one going so far as to caution, "Do not use on genital areas of the body."

> *"The pleasure was so intense it terrified me and I remember telling him I wasn't so sure I liked the mechanical aspect of this machine. He asked me if I wanted him to stop and I wisely said 'no'."* [8]

I once met a woman who had purchased a vibrator on the specific recommendation of her sex therapist. Needless to say, when she read this warning, she was a bit distraught, and I can't blame her. Frankly, I'm not clear just what this company is trying to protect its customers from. I do know that it doesn't want to acknowledge that thousands of women use or intend to use its products for sexual stimulation.

Variable Speed

I am often asked what speed of vibration most people like. My impression is that there is no consistency in this matter. Perhaps one day our stores will have little testers on which we can place a finger or hand to find out what frequency is perfectly in tune with each of us and then we can purchase speed adapters for the vibrators. In the meantime, we have to take what the manufacturers provide.

Fortunately, there are a lot of choices. As mentioned earlier, many battery-operated vibrators have a dial or slide mechanism whereby the speed can be varied. Although most line-voltage vibrators have two fixed speeds, only the Panabrator, a large wand, has a rheostat or variable speed dial. It varies the speed of vibration from very fast to wow!

A conventional light dimmer (the kind designed for use with a table lamp) can be used to lower the speed of motor-driven vibrators but not most coil-operated types. However, manufacturers do not recommend using a rheostat because it stresses the motor too much, causing it to wear out more quickly. Some people, however, use a rheostat regularly with a motor-driven vibrator, suggesting that the motor will burn out only if the power is turned so low that the motor lugs or strains.

Coil-Operated Vibrators

Since the vibrator revolution started with coil-operated devices, I will describe them first. These are the vibrators most likely to be available in your local drug, discount, or department store. You will have to ask for massagers to find them.

A coil-operated vibrator is shaped somewhat like a small hairbrush or hairdryer with the vibrating head at a right angle to the handle. Inside it has an electromagnetic coil, not a motor. The vibrating post (over which plastic attachments are slid) is mounted on a piece of flat metal at the end of the coil. When the 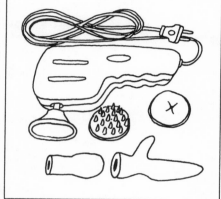 switch is on, it vibrates at 60 cycles/second, the "speed" of the current in the wall. The "high speed" is actually half that fast (about 30 cycles/second), but the vibration feels stronger because the attachment has a longer time to move in each direction and thus moves farther.

Coil-operated vibrators come with four to six plastic attachments of varying flexibility. These are designed for massaging different parts of the body, but you will probably find one or two favorites for use on your genitals.

Almost all of these vibrators are packaged with at least one attachment well suited for clitoral stimulation. Additional attachments are available from companies that sell sex-

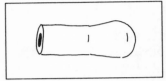

related items. One is what we at Good Vibrations call a Clitickler, a knob-like attachment. A similar attachment is now included with some brand name coil vibrators.

Several four to five inch insertable attachments are also available. Caution must be exercised when using these for internal stimulation, since they sit on a short (½ -¾") shaft, and can wobble loose with

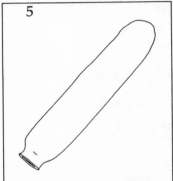

only a little side-to-side pressure. Although the attachment cannot get "lost" in the vagina, the shaft on which it is mounted may become hot if the vibrator has been running a while. And because it can pop off relatively easily, this kind of attachment should never be used for anal stimulation.

Also enjoying a surge of popularity are the Twig and the Come Cup. The Twig is designed for simultaneous clitoral and vaginal stimulation.

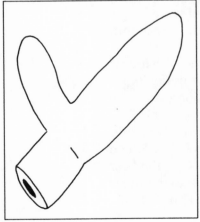

Some women rave about it, while others are disappointed when they try it. The designer had to choose one length and angle for the two tips of the Twig, and that seems to be just right for some women. For others, though, if the longer tip is in the vagina at a comfortable or pleasurable angle, the shorter one is nowhere near the clitoris. The Twig is safe for anal use, because the smaller "branch" will prevent its being inserting too deeply.

The Come Cup is a tulip-shaped attachment designed for stimulating the end of the penis. Reviews of this item are also mixed. Many men find the stimulation too intense, and a few report that the slits that separate the "petals" can pinch if the cup is held around the glans too firmly. On the other hand, some men say the Come Cup lives up to its name admirably.

A few manufacturers make a vibrator that has a heat attachment, or a heat setting. We try to steer people away from using heat vibrators for sex because they can too easily cause minor burns on tender genital tissue. In addition, the user might fall asleep with the hot vibrator touching some part of his or her body.

Heat vibrations are fine, of course, if you use the heat setting or attachment only for your stiff neck or arthritic knee. Just remember to turn off the heat when you want to get yourself hot.

Motor-Driven Vibrators

First reactions to the large wand type vibrator range from "My God, it's so big!" to "So this is what everyone is raving about." The wand-type vibrator, of which the Hitachi Magic Wand is currently the most popular, has a long cylindrical body or handle and a ball-shaped vibrating head attached to the body by a flexible "neck." The two-speed electric motor is attached to a thin shaft which goes

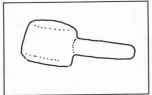

up through the neck into the head. At the top of the shaft, inside the head, is a triangular piece of metal called an off-center or eccentric, which spins and causes the vibration. Because the small motor has moving parts, this kind of vibrator makes a whirring sound.

Wand vibrations are large and slow in comparison to those of the coil-type vibrator. Coil-types actually produce a much smaller,

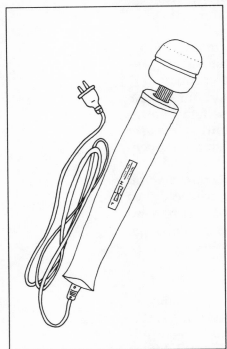

but faster, vibration; that is, the distance the head moves back and forth is much smaller. The amplitude of the vibration, not the frequency, seems to be the quality which leads most people to prefer the wand-type vibrator for massage. They say the vibration is deeper, or stronger. In addition, the relatively larger surface of the vibrating head spreads out the sensation, making the wand preferable for both massage and sexual use.

Some women using the wand-type vibrator experience the relatively slow speed as less driving and overwhelming than the faster motion of the coil-type. One woman said simply, "The vibrations of that little guy [coil-type] are just not in sync with my own vibrations. The speed sets my teeth on edge and makes me feel tense instead of turned on." Most women who have tried both kinds of vibrators do not feel nearly so negative about the coil-type; rather, they find that either kind does quite an adequate job.

The ease with which partners can use these two types of vibrators together is also a factor for many in choosing which to purchase. Aside from the way the vibrations feel to both partners, which is the primary consideration, it is also important to take into account the possibilities for positioning or holding the vibrator so that it is stimulating or comfortable to both people.

> *"One fan pointed out that the only problem she had with vibrators was figuring out what to do for sexual pleasure in a power outage."* [20]

The coil-type's smaller size and silence have been touted as making it the best for partners. These are distinct advantages, but there are two disadvantages as well. Maintaining the "right" position and pressure, which is crucial with this kind of vibrator, can be difficult when there are two bodies to manage instead of one. Also, if the couple is in a face-to-face position, someone's hand has to be between their bodies to hold on to the compact vibrator.

The wand-type's advantage is that couples find the ball-shaped attachment fits nicely between two sets of genitals in all positions but the most traditional missionary position. It works well even in that position if both partners are women. In face-to-face positions, the handle of the vibrator can lie in the groin crease, and be held or moved by a hand that isn't squished between two bodies.

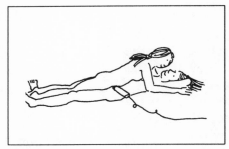

There is an additional advantage of the wand-type vibrator or any good massage vibrator when used by couples. If one or both people are new to vibrators and feeling leery about having this foreign object in bed with them, they can use the vibrator just for massage until they are thoroughly comfortable with it.

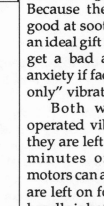

Because the wand vibrator is so good at soothing tense bodies, it is an ideal gift for a person who might get a bad attack of performance anxiety if faced with a "sexual-use-only" vibrator.

Both wand-type and coil-operated vibrators can overheat if they are left on for twenty to thirty minutes or more. Those with motors can actually burn out if they are left on for a long time after the handle is hot to the touch. Manufacturers warn you not to run certain vibrators for more than 25 or 30 minutes; it is wise to abide by their suggestion. If your vibrator gets very hot after only 5 or 10 minutes of operation, it is defective and should be returned to the manufacturer (or retired, depending on its age). Many people own more than one vibrator so they can stay "hot" while one of their vibrators cools off.

The Hitachi Magic Wand has been the best seller at Good Vibrations ever since we opened our doors in 1977. The Hong Kong-made imitations available at some sex shops and through some catalogs can be noisy and are notoriously unreliable. Wands made by Oster and Panasonic (Panabrators) are good quality. The Oster Wand is a little smaller but vibrates faster than the Hitachi. The Panabrator is larger than the Hitachi and vibrates faster as well. It has a rheostat or variable speed control.

Hitachi and one or two other manufacturers also make a double headed vibrator that isn't wand-shaped. Its two spherical heads are mounted side by side on a large case shaped somewhat like the coil-types. This vibrator is superb for massaging the back and neck with the heads placed on either side of the spine, and feels very good on tired arms and legs. It is too heavy and very awkward for many sexual uses with two notable exceptions. Some women respond with great rapidity and intensity when the double header is held pressing on the

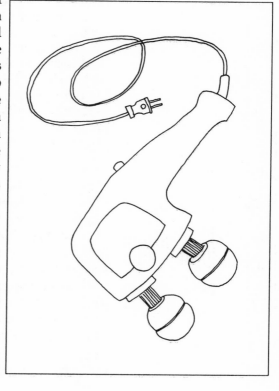

clitoris and anus or on the clitoris and pubic mound at the same time. And some men say the double-header is the perfect masturbation vibrator. All one has to do, they claim, is place the penis between the vibrating heads and hold on for dear life.

Battery-Operated Vibrators

To some readers, perhaps most, the word vibrator brings to mind the cylindrical battery-powered vibrator that is more or less phallic. (The "more or less" is dependent in part on the thing's size, shape, texture, and color, and on the interpretation or fantasy of

the observer.) This is the vibrator most often seen in cartoons in popular men's magazines, as well as in adult bookstores and catalogs, where it can be found in a glorious variety of sizes and shapes. Many vibrators available in "adult" stores and catalogs are designed (rather unsuccessfully, in my opinion) to look and feel like the "real" thing. They are molded from pliant, pink vinyl or latex, complete with "veins," a "glans penis" (head) and, in one case, even a "foreskin."

Battery vibrators sold in novelty stores and through women's magazines are white, hard plastic, of sleek design, and somewhat antiseptic. The fifties-style lady, pictured using this vibrator in the little black and white magazine picture or on the flimsy cardboard box, is inevitably shown snuggling the vibrator up to her plastic smile or daringly applying it with a feather-light touch to her shaven shin. Of course, showing this damsel holding that vibrator anywhere near where it would do any good is out of the question. That would be in bad taste. Unfortunately, in part because no instructions are packaged with this kind of vibrator, many a woman has spent hours shoving it in and out of her vagina, wondering how long the batteries will last and why she doesn't feel much.

I have a personal bias against battery-operated vibrators, but many women use them regularly and happily:

» Those whose preferred method of self-stimulation is the insertion of, or the movement of, an object in the vagina.

» Those who like vaginal insertion as a secondary kind of stimulation, experienced simultaneously with direct clitoral stimulation. (These women often own more than one vibrator — you can guess why.)

» Those who like very gentle vibrations.

» Those who want a vibrator that is very lightweight and easily concealed.

» Those who enjoy anal or anal-rectal stimulation with a vibrator.

» Those who find that a penis-like object in hand or vagina peps up their fantasies.

» Those who live in rural areas with no electricity or who spend a good deal of their time in the great outdoors.

» Those who like to enhance their commute time — a vibrator that plugs into a car cigarette lighter isn't available.

» Those who are fearful of any device that plugs into the wall.

» Those not ready or able to make the financial commitment to a "serious" line-voltage (plug-in) motor- or coil-driven model.

✕ » Those who are given the vibrator by a well-intentioned partner or friend who is committed to the penis-substitute belief or fantasy, too poor to buy the other kind, or simply ill-informed about other options.

✕ » Those who have figured out that just because the vibrator is shaped sort of like a penis, one doesn't have to use it in the way most men enjoy using their penises, that is, by inserting it into a beloved or convenient orifice.

Swedish Massagers

In the same way the word vibrator conjures up a white, hard plastic phallus in many people's minds, the word massager often makes people think of the heavy, squat machine strapped onto the back of the hand, the so-called Swedish massager. Some men know about these from visits to barber shops where the Swedish mas-sager is used for neck and shoulder massage. Both men and women often say that this is the kind Aunt Milly or dear old Granddad kept around. In fact, some of my most aged antiques are of this type.

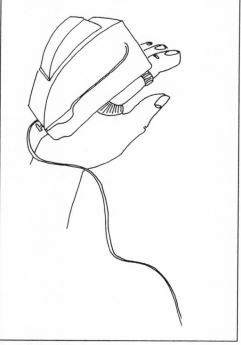

My impression is that very few women use this kind of vibrator for solo sex. Some men find that putting the vibrator on the hand they usually masturbate with enhances the ex-perience; a few are very attached to this way of masturbating. A small number of these men have difficulty coming to orgasm without the vibrator. Swedish or back-of-the-hand mas-sagers allow you to touch your genitals with warm, presumably sensitive hands instead of cold plastic or rubber. And, the vibrations that get through your hand are relatively gentle. However, these are the only advantages.

The disadvantages are that these massagers are quite heavy, the vibration shakes your hand into numbness within just a few minutes, and the spring-like straps have been known to catch pubic hair and do other pinchy things. In summary, a Swedish massager is fine for massage, and can be nifty for sex too — if the hand that's holding it is not your own.

Oddities

WHEN I FIRST WROTE *Good Vibrations* in the mid-seventies, almost all available vibrators fit into one of the categories already mentioned. Now that the plug-in massage vibrators have started to come out of the closet for sexual use, and now that women are taking a more active part in getting what they want sexually, there has been a good deal of hybridization.

There are now plastic, vinyl and latex dildo vibrators which are powered by wall current (with an adapter), solving the problem of batteries that choose to die at the most inauspicious moments. Their quality, however, is not the best. Oster, Wahl and a no-name Hong Kong manufacturer now make rechargeable wand vibrators. They do quite an adequate job for twenty-five to thirty minutes, then require recharging for twelve to fourteen hours. A rechargeable vibrator has great potential for those who like to take their buzzers on picnics, or for those who live in older houses where the only electrical outlet in the room is half a mile away from the bed — or wherever else they may want to play.

I have had many requests for a vibrator which will run on a twelve-volt battery for use in cars, recreational vehicles, and boats, but none is currently available.

In the early seventies, when I was working as a sex therapist with women who were just becoming orgasmic, my colleagues and I dreamed up the idea of a battery-operated vibrator which could be used for clitoral stimulation during intercourse. It had to be small and light-weight with a separate battery pack, and in order for it not to interfere with other sexual activity, we wanted it to be held in place by straps so that neither partner would have to hold it.

I negotiated with a supplier of sexual novelties for what was later to be called the Butterfly, to be manufactured in Hong Kong. Although I had some significant criticism of the early prototype, by the time I saw it the manufacturer had already gone ahead with production. The Butterfly kept its inadequate design for close to ten years, during which time several other sex toy manufacturers copied it, and I did my best to dissociate myself from it.

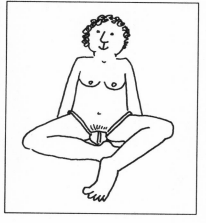

A few years ago the Heart Throb appeared on the scene. It is more compact with a better elastic harness, but alas, it has become no more reliable than the original Butterfly. The Venus Butterfly is the newest incarnation of the Butterfly. Despite the unreliability of these clitoral vibrators, some women have found a regular place for them in their lovemaking.

Eggs

Some battery-powered vibrators are shaped like small eggs or rounded-off bullets. They are attached to a battery pack by a two foot long, thin plastic-coated wire. They are designed for internal vaginal stimulation (although they can be tucked between the labia for labial and clitoral stimulation) and are

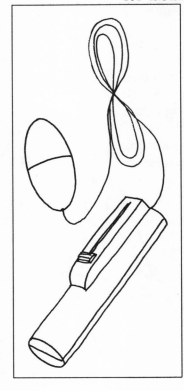

called dancing eggs or vibrating Ben-Wa balls. Jokes are made about "wearing" them to the office to amuse oneself during boring staff meetings. I've heard of, but not seen, a radio-controlled egg designed so one can turn on his or her lover from across a crowded room or elsewhere.

Some women find the sensation provided by vibrating eggs, "bullets" or spheres pleasurable, but usually only because the vibrations bring one's attention to the genital area, and help keep it there. Others find the sensation slightly annoying; a few may experience it as downright uncomfortable, closely akin to the feeling which accompanies a minor urinary tract infection. The fantasy that women will have powerful, multiple orgasms from this kind of stimulation is just that, a fantasy. However, this does not mean that the use of these devices will never result in orgasm, especially if they are used along with other kinds of pleasuring.

Ben-Wa Balls

Now here's a paragraph that's not really about vibrators at all. But since over the years I've had so many questions about Ben-Wa balls, I will discuss them briefly here. Two kinds of non-vibrating toys called Ben-Wa balls are generally available.

One is a set of ½" diameter goldplated ball bearings packaged in pretty little boxes and accompanied by a good deal of hype. The other kind, sometimes known as Duotone Balls, is a set of larger (1½" diameter) plastic spheres attached to each other by a nylon cord for easy removal. Each sphere contains a ½" diameter ball bearing. I don't want to dismiss the fantasy potential of these devices, which is substantial for certain people, but.....

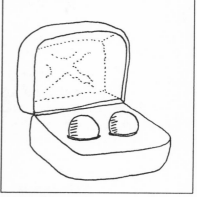

The smaller "gold" balls cannot be felt at all by most women except, perhaps, if they are in the vagina during intercourse. It is not true that they roll around inside. Remember, the unaroused vagina is not a gaping cavern, but a potential space, much like a mouth that is closed. When the larger hollow spheres are inserted, they do not move either, but movement of the heavy balls inside can be felt if the woman wearing them is doing something very active like jogging or vigorous dancing. The sensation is, at best, subtle. A word of caution: either of these toys will set off the metal detector at the airport. No real problem if they are in your purse or suitcase; *big* nuisance and embarrassment if they're in your vagina!

It is not easy to sort out the mythology of these balls from the historical reality. My best information suggests that three to four hundred years ago, hollow spheres made of an ivory-like bone were inserted into the vagina during intercourse by some Japanese women to enhance the experience. These balls did not have mercury or anything else inside them; they were rarely, if ever, used for masturbation; they were not used by women in rocking chairs (unknown in Japan at the time); and presumably, used by themselves, they did not produce orgasm.

Buying a Vibrator

IF VIBRATORS ARE NEW to you then talking with friends about them is helpful. Starting these conversations will be difficult for some people but the payoff, especially in terms of what you learn about yourself, should be substantial. If you have a friend who has a vibrator, borrow it and try it out before going shopping. Whether or not you like your friend's favorite toy, the conversation necessary to arrange the loan will be liberating and enlightening for both of you.

Stores

In some communities, department, discount, and drug stores may have a small selection of vibrators — two or three kinds or brands at the most. They can usually be found with other small electrical appliances, especially blow dryers, or in the cosmetics, housewares or notions departments.

Before you buy, ask to test the strength of the vibrations. Of course, you can't be sure from the sensation on your hand or face how a certain vibrator will feel on your genitals, but you can feel how strong it is, how heavy it is to hold, and how much noise it makes. If you can't decide between a stronger and a weaker one, opt for the stronger; you can always use it through your clothing or a towel at first. Since different stores usually carry different brands, you will probably want to look around before deciding.

If you are shopping for your vibrator at a department store, you may worry that the clerk will want to know what you plan to use it for. Horrors! But, chances are you'll never even get the hint of such a question. And if you do, you can always tell a lie — maybe something about lower back pain or a pulled muscle — if it will help you survive the traumatic experience.

The so-called "adult" bookstore presents a different atmosphere. The selection is small, the prices are high, and the quality of the merchandise is generally poor. While some women have been treated courteously, others have found their experience to be somewhat degrading. When one woman friend of mine went shopping for a vibrator in such an establishment, the salesman said, "Boy, you must really need it bad, sweetie." If you are a woman who wants to find out what's available at one of these places and you're not familiar with its reputation, send in a male friend first or go in with him or another woman.

Home Parties

In the late 1970s, an East Coast woman started at-home parties to sell lingerie and a few sex toys to women whom she (correctly) believed would be embarrassed to shop in adult bookstores. Into the early eighties, these home pleasure parties flourished. At one time there were close to a thousand women running home parties independently or as sales reps for larger companies. This activity has slowed considerably over the past few years, in part because it is now easier to buy sexy lingerie and even a few sex toys in regular stores and boutiques, but probably more because the women running the parties found that they were not lucrative enough.

Unfortunately, many sales reps are often poorly informed about human sexuality and ill-equipped to handle the questions and concerns that inevitably arise when a group of women starts talking openly about sex. More often than not, the manner in which the products are presented, and the information which accompanies them, reflect the attitude that sex is to be talked about only in a joking or sensational way. These presentations often focus primarily on what arouses men, not women. Furthermore, the parties are usually directed to affluent, partnered, heterosexual women; they do not appeal to many feminists, particularly if they happen to be lesbian or bisexual.

> *"This was the beginning of an emotional involvement with a vibrator whom I named 'Big Mac' .... One night Big Mac and I sneaked up on my clitoris, which was under a towel that was folded over at least four times. Just as I feared, instant ecstasy."* [8]

There are a few individual women and small companies who are training their reps conscientiously, presenting only well-made and carefully selected products, and providing a truly educational experience for partygoers. If you live in a suburban or urban area, with a little snooping around you may be able to find out who is doing parties and where, although there are many fewer to choose from than there were in the early 1980s. Most party plans sell books, lotions, oils and other sensual supplies as well as vibrators; some heavily promote lingerie. If you decide to seek out a vibrator at a home party instead of at a store or through the mail, ask in advance for a brief rundown of the products and presentation so you will know what to expect.

Mail Order Catalogs

Another way to buy a vibrator is through the mail. Our mail order business at Good Vibra-

tions has developed from our retail store. People from out of town came to visit the store with their San Francisco friends, then got back home and wrote or called us to order items they wished they'd bought while they were here. We decided to create a catalog, which carries not only several of the vibrators described in this book, but also dildos, harnesses, massage oils and lotions, ostrich feathers and books.

If you want to order from a catalog, there are a few reputable companies that will ship quickly and reliably and stand behind their products. If they give you some suggestions about how to use their products, as we do, that's a plus. The Postal Service is very precise about how mail order companies must fulfill their obligations to their customers and will send you their guidelines if asked.

As mentioned earlier, the Sears catalog carries several models of vibrators, so if you're shy about requesting a sexy mail order catalog, you have another option. No one need ever be without a vibrator!

Vibrators: A User's Manual

IT FEELS GOOD TO PUT a vibrator on most parts of your body — shoulders, neck, lower back, thighs, rear end, face, hands, feet (if you're not too ticklish) and belly. But then, you didn't buy this book to find about those uses. You want to know how to masturbate with the vibrator, right? Well, here goes.

Doing What Feels Good

You can lie down, sit up, stand, kneel, squat, or do yoga postures while using it. Any way you hold your arms or legs is fine. You can move the vibrator, or yourself, or both, or neither. Women can hold the vibrator directly on the clitoris, on or to the side of the clitoral hood, on the mons (the mound of flesh over the pubic bone), on the labia and around the anus or vaginal opening. Dildo-shaped vibrators can be inserted into the vagina or anus. Never put a vibrator (or for that matter, a finger or a penis) into your vagina after it has been in your (or anyone else's) anus, without washing it first. Bacteria natural to the intestinal tract can cause unpleasant infections in the vagina.

> *"How had I reached the age of 33 without ever trying a vibrator? Why isn't it more common-place? Sex educators talk so much about masturbation — but I never heard of anyone suggesting vibrators for women....I thought, every mother should tell her daughter about them; books on sexuality should explain their use."* letter received from a Good Vibrations customer

If you use your vibrator (or any other sex toy) for vaginal or anal insertion *and* if you use it with more than one steady partner, it is a good idea to use a condom on it to prevent the spread of sexually transmitted diseases. Washing the toy with soap and water takes longer but is just as effective as using a condom, unless the toy has a porous surface or seams, nooks and crannies where stuff could get trapped.

You can stroke the genitals as fast or as slowly as you like, or simply press the vibrator lightly or firmly against one spot. You will probably find that as you become aroused your sensations will change. Some people want to speed up and/or increase pressure as they get more turned on; others feel the opposite desire, to slow down and/or lighten up.

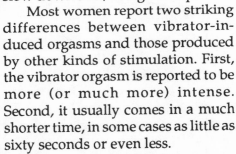

Most women report two striking differences between vibrator-induced orgasms and those produced by other kinds of stimulation. First, the vibrator orgasm is reported to be more (or much more) intense. Second, it usually comes in a much shorter time, in some cases as little as sixty seconds or even less.

Some women who have never had more than one orgasm per session will find that with a vibrator they can have one or several more before going off to slumberland or getting up to go to work. Some women stay highly aroused between these two or more orgasms; others don't, but with continued stimulation find themselves getting turned on once again. Most women who have previously had multiple orgasms find that they can have even more per session; sometimes they use another masturbation method for the first few and a vibrator for the rest. On the other hand, the intensity of the first vibrator orgasm may cause a multi-orgasmic woman to feel like resting instead of continuing as she might otherwise do.

If you feel pretty sure that one is your limit, try this with your vibrator. After your one regular orgasm and a rest of no more than ten to fifteen seconds, start moving or holding the vibrator near or on your most sensitive spot, continue to breathe deeply and easily, and see what happens. If at first you feel numb or a little oversensitive, keep breathing and moving your hips for a while, and chances are that your arousal will increase and you will have another or maybe several more orgasms. Of course, if the stimulation is actually painful, ease up on the pressure or move the vibrator to a different area of your genitals for a while.

> *"[Some] women using the electric vibrator [can] achieve up to fifty orgasms in a single session....From the standpoint of normal physiological functioning, these women exhibit a healthy, uninhibited sexuality — and the number of orgasms attained, a measure of the human female's orgasmic potentiality."* [17]

The only real difference between using the vibrator and using your hand(s) to masturbate is that the vibrator moves faster and has more endurance. It won't change the ways and places you like to be stimulated.

Care and Feeding of Your Vibrator

The only thing that you need to feed your vibrator is a safe and consistent supply of electricity — or fresh batteries, if that's what it prefers.

Never immerse your vibrator in water, even when it is not plugged in. Simply wipe it clean with a damp cloth and soap. Plastic attachments can, of course, swim in soapy water. Some people like to put a condom over the working end of the vibrator or attachment. Generally, however, this is unnecessary unless the vibrator is going to be used by more than one person in a single session.

The most common problem plug-in vibrators experience after some months or years of use is that they start to buzz intermittently and then quit working altogether. The cause of this demise is almost always a short in the cord right at the place where it enters the vibrator. If you can repair a lamp or toaster cord, or have a friend who can, you are in luck. Most plug-in vibrators can be taken apart so you can get at that part of the cord to splice it. There is usually no need to replace the cord altogether.

You can do three things to prevent short-in-the-cord mishaps. First, don't wiggle your vibrator around too much when you are using it. Second, don't sit or lie on your vibrator with the cord bent and mashed under you. Finally, don't pick up your vibrator by the cord. (Well, okay, you can be forgiven if you have to do this once or twice a year in an emergency.)

As a coil vibrator ages, the attachments sometimes loosen, causing them to rattle. This ruins the coil's justly-praised silence, one of the characteristics for which you probably bought it in the first place. You can solve the problem by wrapping a small rubber band around the shaft of the vibrator and pushing the attachment down firmly until at least a bit of the rubber band is wedged between the shaft and the attachment.

If you have a dead battery-operated vibrator which doesn't revive with new batteries, you can try bending any visible metal parts to ensure that the contacts are in fact making contact. Beyond that, the only future for it is a decent burial or a quick, terminal trip to the trash can. You can take it apart, but that is tantamount to irrevocable destruction.

Women and Vibrators

MOST WOMEN WHO HAVE their first orgasm with a vibrator have never before had adequately intense stimulation. There is nothing abnormal about requiring intense stimulation to trigger an orgasm. Many people, for example, enjoy eating spicy food or turning up the volume on their stereos. Nobody really believes someone is weird for preferring these pleasurable sensations at above-average intensity.

If You've Never Had An Orgasm

First, make friends with your genitals. Look at them in the mirror and say hello with your fingers. Use some saliva or water-based lubricant for slipperiness. Find out which areas are especially sensitive to your touch and which are less so. Explore different kinds of touch, varying the speed and pressure. Don't expect to have an orgasm right away. It may take as long as several weeks for your body to learn or relearn how to receive pleasure from your own touch.

Now, start touching yourself with your vibrator. If it has two "speeds" try them both. You may want to touch your belly, thighs, and hips first to see how it feels. When you first put the vibrator on your genitals, you may choose to use a towel or cloth between you and the vibrator. Or, you may want to hold the vibrator directly on your clitoris, on the hood covering the clitoris, or on the mons (the fatty mound covering your pubic bone.) If your vibrator is cylindrical (the battery-operated kind), or if it is an electric vibrator

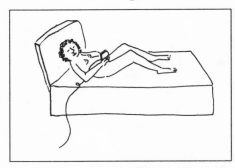

with a long (insertable) attachment, you can insert it into your vagina and/or move it gently in and out.

Although insertion may feel very good to you, it is improbable that you will become aroused enough to have an orgasm unless you stimulate the clitoral area at the same time with your fingers or another vibrator. Remember, there are few nerve endings inside the vagina that respond to light touch or friction. The entrance to the vagina and the inner lips may be very sensitive, however, and they can be reached comfortably with any vibrator.

If you are a male partner of a woman who has never had an orgasm, the fact that you are reading this book suggests that you are supportive of her using a vibrator to enhance her sexual pleasure. Please let her introduce you to her new-found responses only when she feels ready to do so. If she is comfortable talking about it, encourage her to do so; if not, don't push her. The first few orgasms — even high levels of arousal without orgasm — can be very overwhelming to a woman who has never experienced them. Also, recognize how unlikely it is that she will start having orgasms with intercourse right away. It is possible that she will never become orgasmic with intercourse. However, if either of you thinks that there is only one "right" way to have an orgasm, please let me know what the "wrong" way is. I believe there is no such thing.

If You Get Aroused Easily But Can't Get Over the Top

Tease yourself. Stop and start again. Play with your arousal level. Stop "trying." This is supposed to be pleasurable, not hard work. Notice how much you can control your arousal level by changing the stimulation. Then see if you can become more aroused while keeping the stimulation constant. If you enjoy sexual fantasies, let your mind go with whatever happens. If fantasy is not your thing, focus on the way all the parts of your body — not just your genitals — feel.

Remember, some degree of muscular tension goes along with sexual arousal. Focus on it and alternate exaggerating the tension and then relaxing. Move gently or vigorously, then hold very still. Play with your breath, too. Try slow, deep, regular breaths and then short, shallow, panting breaths. Then hold your breath for a few seconds and let it go with a big sigh.

> "When a woman is new to vibrator sex, she may experience any number of responses. One friend reported that the first time she used her vibrator, she had the most intense orgasm of her life, but it was over before she knew what had happened. Another said her orgasm was ever so slight, lasting only a second. And yet another woman had to practice patiently for several months before anything sexual happened." [9]

Spend a little time every day masturbating with your vibrator and hands without the expectation of having an orgasm. It may take twenty to thirty minutes or more at first, and the first few orgasms may take you by surprise. They may be very mild, even disappointing, or very intense. Give yourself time to figure out exactly what unique combination of conditions suits you best.

Vaginal Vibration and the G-Spot

For the past twenty years, women have been rejoicing in the discovery that clitoral stimulation can give them great pleasure and assure them plentiful and reliable orgasms. Scientific studies concluded that there is no such thing as a "vaginal orgasm," that is, an orgasm triggered by vaginal stimulation alone.

"An organic dildo can be made from a cucumber or zucchini....Cucumbers are naturally moist and slippery and have been used in beauty creams for years. One day I was cruising the cucumber bin in a supermarket with such thoughtfulness that a woman standing nearby asked me how I knew which ones were best. I couldn't resist. 'Mainly intuition,' I said. 'I'm picking out a lover for tonight.' She doubled over with laughter as I winked and walked off." [9]

For a good number of years, the word has been that if a woman *is* orgasmic with vaginal stimulation alone (usually meaning intercourse), the real cause is indirect clitoral stimulation incidental to penile thrusting. Since it is impossible to stimulate the vagina during intercourse without stimulating the clitoral area, you can see how difficult it is to sort this out. Nevertheless, the acknowledgement of clitoral orgasms has helped thousands of women who felt themselves to be deficient in their sexual response to feel "normal" again. It has also enabled heterosexual women to feel far less

38

dependent on their partners. In addition, it has helped at least some people understand how two women can be sexual together without using a penis substitute.

Unfortunately — and frankly because we didn't know any better — the experiences of certain women were discounted or disbelieved in the enthusiastic rush to accept new explanations and the "scientific" evidence supporting them. I am referring to those women who have consistently claimed that the orgasms they have during 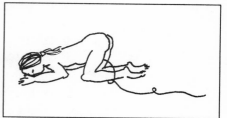 intercourse are significantly different in several ways from those resulting from direct clitoral stimulation.

Also discounted have been the experiences of women who claim they are orgasmic *only* during intercourse and who may even actively dislike direct clitoral stimulation. Finally, for years *no one* believed women who claim that they ejaculate or experience an involuntary expulsion of fluid during coital orgasm or other vaginal or clitoral stimulation. They have been told that they are either lying or suffering from urinary stress incontinence, that is, losing urine at the moment of orgasm because of weakness of the musculature around the urethra.

However, contemporary research about female sexual response will in all probability turn our ideas upside down. This research suggests:

» that women have a small body of prostate-like tissue surrounding the urethra,

» that many women find stimulation of this area (called the Graefenberg spot, or G-Spot) through the anterior (top or front) wall of the vagina by fingers, dildo, or penis to be very pleasurable and arousing, and

» that some women who experience orgasm from this stimulation ejaculate a fluid through the urethra during these orgasms.

The fluid expelled closely resembles male seminal fluid (semen without sperm) in its chemical composition. It may be that many women who at one time experienced such ejaculation have learned to hold back the ejaculate so that it backs up into the bladder. (This phenomenon is called retrograde ejaculation; it is not uncommon in men who have had certain types of prostate surgery.) This attempt to hold back the embarrassing ejaculation may inhibit orgasm altogether, so that these women are no longer orgasmic with vaginal stimulation.

Since a good part of the vibrator explosion is associated with the celebration of clitoral sexuality, vibrators should naturally be a part of any future breakthroughs. Those of us who are vibrator enthusiasts will now want to find out how we can use vibrators for stimulation of the G-Spot and by so doing expand our capacity for arousal and orgasm. Curved attachments now available for several plug-in vibrators, and a curved battery vibrator, are intended as G-Spot stimulators. I have talked with a significant number of women who like and use vibrators *and* who enjoy manual or coital G-Spot stimulation, but the word is not yet in on how well they go together.

It is almost impossible for a woman to give herself effective G-Spot stimulation using her finger(s). It can be done if she uses an object such as a straight vibrator in her vagina, but she may find it awkward. For this reason, experimenting with vibrator stimulation of the G-Spot might best be tried with a partner at first. Depending on the shape of your vibrator, you can try pressing or rubbing the G-Spot through the vaginal wall, or from the outside, by pressing the vibrator firmly downward on the lower abdomen right at the pubic hair line. Some women find this sensation irritating if they are insufficiently aroused. Stop if any of your experiments result in prolonged feelings of urinary urgency or any pain. This is not a contest in sexual versatility. You are seeking pleasure, and the search should not be uncomfortable.

Vibrators can be very important in optimizing women's newly discovered sexual responses. The popularity of vibrators has increased dramatically during recent years, and is still on the upswing, as more and more women learn more about the pleasure potential of masturbation and various forms of non-coital stimulation by partners. The search for the "look-ma-no-hands" coital orgasm is now driven more by curiosity than by desperation.

Using the Vibrator for Anal/Rectal Stimulation

Battery-operated, dildo-type vibrators are often used for anal stimulation. Many men find that stimulating the anal opening, the lower rectum, and the prostate (through the wall of the rectum) with a vibrator is very pleasurable. Although women have no prostate, they are increasingly exploring anal stimulation both by themselves and with partners.

The anus is one of the most sensitive areas of the body, hence it has great potential for pleasure. Around the anus are many nerve endings that can be stimulated both by friction and also by muscular contractions. These nerve endings seem to become more sensitive during sexual excitement. Many women and men enjoy the sensation of the anus contracting around something, such as a finger, vibrator or penis.[15]

To become more comfortable with anal eroticism, start with gentle finger stimulation. Use plenty of lubricant because the anus has virtually no natural lubrication, and be sure fingernails are clipped very short and smooth. If you are doing this with a partner and you are not absolutely confident that *neither* of you has or has been exposed to a sexually transmitted disease, use a snugly fitting finger cot — which is essentially a latex sheath — or wear a rubber glove.

After you feel very comfortable with the insertion of a finger, try the vibrator. Make sure you select one that is long enough for you or your partner to keep a good grip on it.

First just touch and stroke the outside of the anus. Then when you feel ready, insert the vibrator. Move the vibrator in, and especially out, very slowly at first until you feel thoroughly familiar and comfortable with the sensation.

You can also experiment with a vibrator especially designed for anal/rectal stimulation. These are called plugs or butt plugs and are designed in such a way that once inserted they will stay in place while the wearer engages in other activities, sexual or otherwise. They widen in the middle and taper near the base to keep them from slipping out. More important, they have a flange at the base to keep them from going in too far.

For more guidance on this subject, get a copy of Jack Morin's *Anal Pleasure and Health: A Guide for Men and Women* (Yes Press).

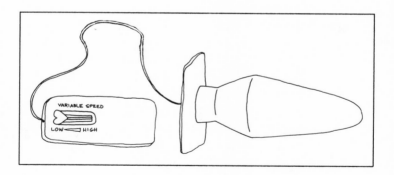

Men and Vibrators

IT IS A POPULAR BELIEF that vibrators are used almost exclusively by women. Theoretically, this doesn't make sense. If men, like women, enjoy a wide range of stimuli (and we know that they do), then why shouldn't a vibrator be another potential source of sexually arousing stimulation?

The problem with this theory is that it fails to take into account social inhibitors and the attitudes that many men have about vibrators. Some of these negative ideas men and women share: vibrators are too mechanical; they may be habit-forming; masturbation isn't too swell an idea in any form.

Other beliefs seem to belong almost exclusively to men. One of these is the fear of appearing feminine either to oneself or to others. Vibrators have for so long been thought of as sex toys for women that some men react defensively to the suggestion they might enjoy using the vibrator for themselves. Some men, when asked if they have ever used a vibrator, will happily describe the times they've used a vibrator on a woman, but would never ever admit having considered using it for self-stimulation or inviting a partner to stimulate them with it.

Some heterosexual men believe that only homosexual men use vibrators, and then only for anal stimulation. That means a few may

> *"Powerful vibrations can be very effective for bringing on an erection. Although few men report the ability to climax with the vibrator used alone (possibly due to lack of patience), most men report strong and satisfying orgasms combining a variety of techniques, especially vibratory stimulation along with manual caressing of the penis."* [19]

even believe that if they use a vibrator they are or will become homosexual.

Some men are negative about masturbation in any form. Of course, some women feel this way as well. However, men usually start masturbation earlier in life and usually experience more overt negativity about it from parents and other adults. Therefore, they are somewhat more likely than women to view adult masturbation as a bad habit. Whatever the reasons, it seems that a majority of women who feel very negative about masturbation simply don't do it. By contrast, it seems most men do masturbate, regardless of whether they feel good about it. And the man who feels that masturbation is a bad habit is not likely to seek out anything to enhance that experience.

Virtually all men who masturbate are orgasmic. Therefore, many men have difficulty understanding how a woman cannot always come when masturbating manually. Since men's usual way of masturbation is 100% reliable, they will often say, "I don't need a vibrator." These men don't think of the vibrator as an enhancer or alternative; they think of it as a crutch for certain women who cannot have orgasms without it. Moreover, the dildo vibrators that most men know of or visualize when they think of vibrators seem designed to stimulate a woman's vagina, not the male genitals.

> *"Picking up an electric vibrator, I put it in his hands, turned on the switch, and guided it over his limp penis until I saw a faint smile on his lips. Later, Al [reported] how amazed he was to have had a second orgasm with a vibrator and a soft-on."* [9]

Some men have tried a vibrator for self-stimulation but do not continue to use it after one or a few brief attempts. Of these, some are probably men who do not masturbate with any regularity for a variety of reasons. I have talked with others who, though eager to try self-stimulation with a vibrator, have been disappointed when it didn't "do anything" for them. Here are some common reactions:

» "It was too fast and it just didn't feel good at all."
» "It felt good but I didn't get an erection or get aroused."
» "I felt turned on and I got an erection but I couldn't come; I had to turn off the vibrator and go back to my usual method when I wanted to come."
» "After I got an erection it started to feel boring and sort of numb, so I quit."
» "I eventually ejaculated but it took me so long and seemed like such hard work that I probably won't do it again."

Some of these responses reflect the goal orientation so prevalent in the sexual attitudes of most of us. We tend to reject that which only feels good in favor of that which arouses us or gives us orgasms. We forget that unless we learn about, acknowledge and focus on that which feels good, sexual experience is reduced to a mechanical exercise or an athletic performance.

If you are a man and have not had an experience with a vibrator or have been disappointed when you experimented before, and if you want to check out the pleasure potential of the vibrator further, you can follow some of the suggestions for use given earlier for women. In addition, consider the following:

» Some men do not get erections at all or get only partial erections when they stimulate themselves with a vibrator. Nevertheless, according to some individual reports, this in no way affects the sense of arousal. In other words, you may feel just as aroused as you normally would with a full erection.

» It sometimes takes a long time for a man to come with a vibrator. Some men have several orgasms during this relatively long arousal period before ejaculating.

» If you are not using a device that surrounds the penis, you may want to cup your hand around your penis so that the vibrator touches your hand, making a ring of sensation rather than a spot. Another way to spread the sensation is to press your penis against your abdomen with the vibrator.

» If the vibration doesn't feel good directly on the penis, experiment with holding the vibrator or stroking with it at the base of the penis, on the scrotum, on the perineum, around the anal opening or against the pubic bone.

» If you want to stimulate the prostate through the wall of the rectum, remember to use a butt plug, or a battery-operated dildo vibrator which is long enough so that you (or your partner)

47

won't lose hold of it. Some men have experienced ejaculation from prostate stimulation in a doctor's office, but do not describe it as particularly pleasurable. In a more sensual setting, and perhaps with the aid of fantasy, anal/prostate stimulation can trigger orgasm as well as ejaculation. G-Spotter attachments for wand vibrators are also great for this.

» If you choose to try anal stimulation with a vibrator, you can, of course, combine it either with your usual form of masturbation or stimulation of your genitals by a partner.

Recently men have been talking about having multiple orgasms; a few have always claimed that this is their experience. How vibrator stimulation affects or might affect the male orgasmic capacity is not known.

Also not known is how men who are reliably orgasmic with vibrator stimulation describe their orgasms in comparison to other orgasms. So far, men haven't talked much about such things to me or probably even to each other.

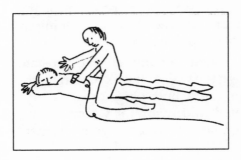

Water and Vibrators

COMMON SENSE DICTATES against using a plug-in vibrator (or any electrical appliance) in the bathtub, shower, swimming pool, jacuzzi or other watery venues. However, these are good places to experiment with getting turned on by a fast-running stream of water. The faucet in your tub, a bidet, the inlet of a swimming pool or jacuzzi, a hand-held shower massager, and a water pick (designed for cleaning teeth) are all worth a try.

Be *very* careful with the water pick and shower massager. They push water out at a pretty high velocity, which can be painful. *Never* direct a forceful stream of water into your vagina. It is possible to force water and air bubbles through the cervix into the uterine cavity, where they can cause no end of serious trouble.

A woman who lubricates copiously, urinates a little, or ejaculates when she becomes highly aroused or has an orgasm, might be concerned about getting a shock, shorting out or rusting her electric vibrator. I've never heard of this happening, but if it makes you feel more relaxed, hold the body or motor of the vibrator off to the side or up toward your belly button so it won't get wet.

Vibrators — Who's the Boss?

SOME PEOPLE WORRY that they will become addicted to the vibrator. If an addiction is a habit that is in some way harmful to a person, then the words 'vibrator' and 'addiction' don't even belong in the same sentence. Some people do get so accustomed to vibrator stimulation that for a time they enjoy it more than any other stimulation. But those who have had orgasms in other ways usually continue to do so with no difficulty. A few people eventually give up other kinds of sex play with themselves and with partners and head straight for the machine. If this describes you and you want to get unhooked, this is what you can do.

> "Of all my addictions, the vibrator is the mildest and least destructive....After I have the food addiction under control, I'll take a look at my vibrator addiction ... until then I can only say it's not fattening, illegal or immoral." [8]

Give yourself some extended time alone and/or with a partner to enjoy non-vibrator sexual activities. If you find yourself trying to have an orgasm, slow down the stimulation, or stop and start again. Pay attention to what feels good and what feels better, and you will start to feel aroused again. If you are with a partner who is stimulating you, ask him or her to slow down, move over or stop when you observe yourself trying to come. Do not expect any orgasm you happen to have with manual, oral or coital stimulation to feel the same as those you have become accustomed to with the vibrator.

Chances are these orgasms will be somewhat less intense at first. After a while, if you don't use the vibrator at all, your responses

50

will be back to what they were before you started with the vibrator.

Of course, if you have become orgasmic since using a vibrator, you will maintain that status. Rejoice, you are no longer non-orgasmic, and you got there by yourself. Celebrate your new independence, and don't let a sexual partner or anyone else convince you that your reliance on your vibrator is the least bit unhealthy.

A few women have rarely or never experienced any pleasure they could label sexual until they discovered the vibrator. You may think that such a woman is more likely than others to get 'stuck' on her vibrator. Not so. Generally, vibrator use gives this woman confidence and the knowledge that her body *is* responsive, and she can go on to discover new ways of turning herself on.

Some sex therapists recommend weaning oneself from the vibrator, but I am not one of them. Some women have done this successfully, others have tried and failed. Since I am not a believer in weaning, I am not a good source of information on how to go about attempting it. To me, it implies that the best way to reach orgasm is the "natural" way, that the vibrator is a crutch you shouldn't need when you grow up, and/or that it's not a good habit.

Some people feel that if they enjoy masturbation with the vibrator, they might mas-

> *"There are some myths and concerns circulating about vibrators which probably prevent some women from trying them out. The most common myth is that a vibrator provides sensations which are so marvelous and sinfully gratifying that it will replace your partner or make it impossible for you to come using anything but a vibrator. This is a half-truth .... we don't worry about someone getting addicted to oral sex."[5]*

turbate too much. Since the 1940s we've been reading that masturbation is all right as long as a person (in the books it's usually a male adolescent person) doesn't do it "to excess." For years I turned eagerly to the chapter on masturbation in each new book on sex, hoping it would tell me how much was excessive. It never did! You will know it's too much for you if you often find yourself masturbating when you would rather be doing something else.

An alternative to getting unhooked is to decide that you feel okay about being a vibrator enthusiast and then buzz off as much as you want. Unlike some other addictions, this one has no known detrimental physical side effects. In any event, just as one cannot blame food for compulsive overeating, one cannot blame a vibrator for compulsive masturbation — if such a thing does exist.

Sex researchers and counselors working with women are finding that the more times a woman experiences sexual response, the more reliable her response becomes. In fact, I believe that if girls discovered their clitorises in infancy and masturbated throughout their lives, as most boys and men do, they would experience fewer difficulties with sexual response as adults.

I would urge both men and women to let go of the demands they place on themselves about having an orgasm or having a certain number of orgasms each time they become aroused (alone or together).

If you're not worried about vibrator addiction, but your partner is, invite him or her to read this book, especially this section, and then talk over his or her concerns. Then, see if your partner is actually worried that you will start to enjoy solo sex more than sex with him or her. If so, invite your partner to be with you during a masturbation session or start practicing the activities suggested on pages 58-60.

Even sex therapists who routinely prescribe masturbation as therapy for orgasm concerns often do not see self-pleasuring as a worthy end in itself. So it's not surprising that partners who have some uneasiness over their own masturbation may be less than enthusiastic about yours. Remember that no modern society, even late twentieth century American society, has bestowed any value on masturbation.

But My Therapist Said...

Over the years, hundreds of women have purchased vibrators from us on the specific recommendation of their therapists. However, not long ago a Good Vibrations customer wrote to tell us that her therapist had instructed her to throw away her vibrator. She and her husband were being seen because he had difficulty maintaining an erection. My guess is that the therapist was concerned that this woman would masturbate during the course of the therapy and then find it harder to become aroused during intercourse once her husband's situation was resolved.

It is very common in couples sex therapy to prescribe a short

"We use electric stimulation for all sorts of treatments. Why not use it to develop the sensory pathway from clitoris to consciousness....So many inhibitions have been built up that it takes a most vigorous electric force generated in the receptor nerve endings to break through the synapses and finally reach the level of consciousness." [7]

term ban on intercourse or on whatever sexual activity seems to be causing the most anxiety. It is rare, however, that a sex therapist will ask couples to abstain from all sexual activity, including masturbation (as this therapist did). As a matter of fact, masturbation practice is often recommended as a way for each partner to learn more about his or her own sexual response.

Unfortunately, some therapists who support masturbation are not equally enthusiastic about vibrator use. Fortunately, for every therapist who thinks vibrators are habit-forming, dozens of others see them as pleasure enhancing and, consequently, therapeutic.

You're in Control

Although your vibrator moves fast, it doesn't have a mind of its own. The hand that holds it is always in control. If you doubt that, experiment by moving it onto and away from your most sensitive area, starting and stopping, or teasing yourself. Alternate the vibrator with your fingers, moving it at different speeds, and with varying amounts of pressure. A good basic rule of thumb is: if it doesn't hurt, it won't hurt you ... and it might feel wonderful. In this regard, remember that when a person is highly aroused his or her pain tolerance goes way up. You will want to exercise caution at first if you choose to exert a lot of pressure or rub your vibrator vigorously on your skin or mucous membranes.

> *"If you get off on using your electric massager and start feeling guilty about it, ask yourself why you're afraid of feeling good."* [5]

Can the vibrator numb your genitals or damage nerve endings in some way? Not that we know of. Your clitoris or penis may indeed feel numb after you have held the vibrator on it for some minutes. Slowing down, moving the vibrator off slightly, or stopping for a few minutes and starting again, will almost always bring back pleasurable sensations.

People who like playing with the vibrator for long periods of time may experience a range of sensations including numbness and oversensitivity, as well as warmth, tingliness or throbbing. The genitals are not like the ear. Although loud music or noise can cause permanent hearing loss, lots of genital stimulation, even intense stimulation, does not result in loss of sexual excitability. *Au contraire*, it seems as if the more you use it the better it works!

Vibrators and Your Partner

SOME OF YOU MAY BE fortunate enough to have discovered the joys of vibrators with the full knowledge and enthusiastic involvement of one or more sexual partners.

If the vibrator is new to your partner, or if he or she has expressed negative feelings about vibrator use, you may be reluctant to introduce it into your sex life with this person. It is your responsibility to present your interest in using the vibrator in such a way that it will be well-received. You might be surprised at how suppor-

> *"Whenever I came home, there was my new electric vibrator, waiting faithfully to give me endless hours of pleasure....What saved me from going steady was careful consideration of her shortcomings: all buzz and no conversation, and she never initiated lovemaking."* [9]

55

tive your partner is, especially if you initiate the discussion with the intent of sharing your enthusiasm.

Some heterosexual men are resistant to

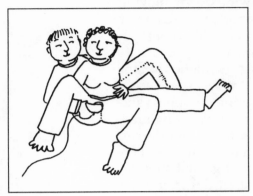

learning about clitoral stimulation in particular. If your partner is one of those men for whom "real sex" begins and ends with penis/vagina intercourse, you may have to go through an educational process to help him understand your reality.

If you are a heterosexual woman who is not orgasmic with penis/vagina intercourse alone (like forty to seventy percent of all women), you may start having orgasms during intercourse as you become more comfortable with stroking your clitoris at the same time. After becoming reliably orgasmic this way, some women want to try taking the hand or vibrator away from the clitoris before they come to see if intercourse alone will take them over the top. Others, delighted with the orgasm just the way it is, don't want to risk missing it even once, just for the sake of experiment. As long as a look-ma-no-hands orgasm is *your* goal, and not your partner's (or someone else's) goal *for* you, pursue it if you like. If you enjoy the vibrator regularly, you may plan occasional or even frequent partnered sex during which you don't use your vibrator. Keeping it handy anyway is very reassuring. It's nice to know that you can pop an extra orgasm or two into the encounter or that you can revive your sexual interest if it flags before you and your partner are ready to call it a night.

Contrary to popular belief, you do not have to be a human pretzel to give yourself clitoral stimulation with or without the vibrator while having intercourse. The missionary position — man on top, woman on the bottom — is probably not the best position for clitoral stimulation, unless your partner wants to position 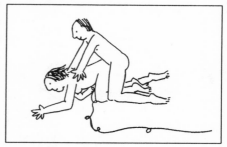 his body at more or less of a right angle to yours instead of parallel to it, so you can reach your clitoris. Most rear entry positions are good except one in which you are flat on your stomach. Woman astride or on top is excellent if you are comfortable in it. A favorite for many couples has the woman on her back, the man on his side, close to and facing her, with both her legs draped over his thighs. In a slight variation, the legs are intertwined in a way that defies description. There are many other options. Your own explorations should be much more fun than reading these few paragraphs.

Who should hold the vibrator? It is often hard for even the most diligent lover to stay in touch with a woman's clitoris with his or her hand or mouth. Unless you like the vibrator

"A vibrator fits into a woman's life wherever and however she wants it to fit in, but it can get in the way of a man-woman relationship if her partner doesn't like it or if she's using it because she's angry and is sending out strong messages that the machine can do something that he can't." [2]

held still while you move against it, better hold it yourself.

If you are a man introducing a vibrator to a reluctant female partner, try to understand her resistance, particularly if you learned about vibrators from a previous woman 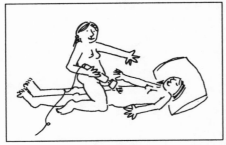 partner who may have been more of a sexual sophisticate. When purchasing a vibrator for such a woman, you would do well to choose one that feels good to you, at least for massage. Then you can bring it to bed as a toy for both of you to enjoy. If you scoff at the idea of enjoying the vibrator yourself, you run the risk of making her feel deficient in some way, as if she needs mechanical assistance while you do not.

If you are a woman who enjoys a vibrator a great deal when masturbating and who wants to "come out of the closet" about your vibrator use, here are some things you can do:

» Have a talk with a friend (not a sexual partner and preferably someone of the same sex) about masturbation and vibrators. Allow yourself to be as explicit as you can in order to learn as much as possible about yourself. Verbally explore not only your attitudes and those of your friend, but also your behavior. If he or she has tried a vibrator or uses one regularly, inquire about and share your experiences with specific techniques. If neither of you has any

58

experience with partnered vibration, brainstorm about what might feel good. If you expect to get a negative reaction when introducing the vibrator, do some worst-case thinking about what your partner might say and role play your assertive response.

» Do the same thing with your lover or spouse. The experience will probably be substantially different. Don't have sex while you are talking; it complicates the discussion. Remember that if your partner is critical of you, he or she is really telling you something about him/herself. If you do get criticism, try to hear, acknowledge and then talk about the feeling(s) lurking behind it. View this as an experiment and remind yourself and your partner that the worst that can happen is that the discussion won't be all that much fun — in which case you probably won't do it again. Most of the time, anticipated negative reactions to vibrators never materialize. Chances are you'll wish you hadn't waited and worried as long as you did.

> "The hostility toward vibrators common to many (but far from all) men is no doubt in part a form of jealousy.... I prefer to think of the vibrator as a helper, rather than a rival. I can add up a column of figures without help — but I'm much more efficient with a calculator." [4]

» Make a date for a vibrator playtime with a cooperative partner. Choose someone who will let you proceed at *your* own pace. Plan some sexual activities for the session that don't involve the vibrator (perhaps some you've enjoyed together before) so that if the vibrator doesn't make both of you feel good, the session will be fun anyway. Take lots of breaks. If you have a vibrator that is good for all-over-body massage, take this opportunity to allow your partner to pleasure you *non*-sexually with it for part or all of one or several sessions. After the playtime is over, have a talk about how it was for each of you.

» Get your vibrator out of the bottom drawer and keep it out in the open by your bed. Start thinking of it as a useful household appliance and keep it handy.

» Consider adding a new kind of vibrator to your collection and go shopping for the new toy with your partner. Or, select one from a mail order catalog together.

» Don't forget vibrators when you are deciding on a gift for a parent, sibling, relative or friend. Even a confirmed vibrator enthusiast can always use one more.

Health Considerations and Special Uses

ALL VIBRATORS AND MASSAGERS sold in the United States have for years been labeled as follows: "Do not use on swollen areas or on unexplained calf pain." The latter part of this warning relates to the risk of shaking loose a blood clot (embolus) which could travel elsewhere in the body, possibly causing serious damage or even death.

You will see some battery-operated vibrators labeled "sold as a novelty only." The manufacturer wants to be sure you know that he or she is making no therapeutic claims for his product, because if he does, it becomes subject to Food and Drug Administration (FDA) regulation. When the FDA was drawing up regulations in the late 1970s, it received comments suggesting that it should not waste Federal tax money to regulate genital vibrators. I agree, and apparently so does the FDA, because they are concerned only with genital vibrators "intended and labeled for therapeutic use."[10]

Occasionally a physician will recommend the non-sexual use of a vibrator for a medical problem. If you have a painful or otherwise uncomfortable condition that you think would be relieved by vibration or another kind of massage, check with your doctor first to be sure there is no risk in using a vibrator.

Pregnant women have reported that vibration is very comforting both for stretched-out bellies and back aches late in pregnancy. Orgasms, whether induced by the vibrator or any other source of stimulation, are not contraindicated for most pregnant women and some find that, especially during the last few months of pregnancy, a vibrator is very handy. Women who have a history of pre-term labor or those who have any indication that their labor might start too early should *not* use vibrators on their bellies, backs or genitals. The vibration could trigger premature uterine contractions.

Keep a battery vibrator handy, though, for the first few months of your baby's life. Parents report that some fussy babies can be calmed with a gentle back massage *à la vibrator*, or by placing the vibrator, wrapped in a towel, in the crib.

Recently, some hospitals have been buying large numbers of small battery-powered vibrators for the neonatal nursery. They are used on the backs of tiny infants to help the babies cough up fluid that collects in the lungs. We've often wondered if the hospital staff have found out about the recreational use of these vibrators, too.

Some speech therapists also use little vibrators to help their patients develop awareness and improve function of the small muscles around the mouth. Therapists and

62

teachers who work with deaf and blind children have reported that vibrators can provide a new range of sensation for kids whose interaction with their environment is significantly impaired by their disability.

Adults with certain physical disabilities have discovered vibrators to be a real boon to their sexual explorations. People with limited genital sensation sometimes find that a strong vibrator can "get through" to them when hand stimulation cannot. This may be especially important for diabetics who are experiencing some neuropathy (early nerve damage). Many people whose hands and arms tire easily or those who have limited strength or mobility in their arms and hands find the vibrator very useful in helping them become sexually independent. Sexual independence is a right that belongs to all of us, whatever our degree of physical ability.

> *Vibrators are so perfect for orgasms that it's easy to forget how wonderful they are for massage. Whenever you vibrate you are stimulating the flow of blood to the area, a marvelous health and beauty treatment for the entire body."* [9]

... And She (or He) Buzzed Happily Ever After

INSTRUCTORS OF HUMAN SEXUALITY classes are sometimes accused of leaving "love" out of their courses. A book like this may engender a similar reaction from some of its readers. I believe that sex and love vary independently. One may be a superb lover in the sense that he or she always knows what to do to arouse a partner; this says little or nothing about his or her ability to initiate, build or maintain a loving, intimate relationship, be it casual or committed. Conversely, in many intensely intimate relationships, sex is not terribly important to either person.

This book, other sexual self-awareness materials, vibrators and other sex toys will not make love happen. Where there is sex without love they will make little or no difference in the emotional climate. Where there is love, they may enhance or liven up the sex by augmenting verbal and physical communication and contact.

It is currently popular to stress the necessity of loving oneself in order to be able to love another. And, in spite of cultural prohibitions against selfishness and putting oneself first, many people are finding that as their self-esteem improves, their relationships become much more satisfying. In spite of this, masturbation, or making love to oneself, is still seen as a second- or third-rate sexual activity compared to having sex with someone else. Indeed, those who say that their self-sexuality is a valid and important component of their overall sexual expression risk being viewed as abnormal, isolated and self-centered. Never fear. Many men and women are enthusiastic about masturbation; no one I know always prefers it to shared sex. And most say that each one enhances the other.

We often use "love" as a euphemism for sexual activity. In so doing, we can, if we choose, avoid talking about sex at all. As long as we avoid talk about sex, we are likely to maintain negative attitudes about it. Becoming affirmative about sex inevitably changes our perspective about the functions of sex in our individual makeup and in our relationships. It frees up energy previously expended in keeping up the pretense that we are "nice people" who lack interest in whatever it is that might trigger our lust.

What part can a vibrator play in freeing your sexual energy and helping you become more sex-affirming? First, you will learn something about yourself if you can observe how your current beliefs affect your decision to obtain a vibrator. Second, you can start a new kind of discussion with a friend or lover using vibrators as a topic. Finally, you can bring an entirely new, and most people agree different, sensation into both your self-loving and shared sexual experiences. While you are at it, don't forget to HAVE FUN. That's really what it's all about.

Selected Readings

1. Barbach, Lonnie. *For Yourself: The Fulfillment of Female Sexuality*. New York: Signet, 1975.

2. Barbach, Lonnie (quoted in Safran *Esquire* article).

3. Brecher, Edward M. *The Sex Researchers*. San Francisco: Specific Press, 1969, 1979.

4. Brecher, Edward M. "The Vibrator: A Man's Best Friend." *Forum*, June 1978.

5. Califia, Pat. *Sapphistry: The Book of Lesbian Sexuality*. Tallahassee: Naiad Press, 1988.

6. Castleman, Michael. *Sexual Solutions: A Guide for Men and the Women Who Love Them*, revised edition. New York: Simon & Schuster, 1980, 1983, 1989.

7. Clark, LeMon. "Specificity and Effectiveness of Sex Therapy." presented at the International Congress of Sexology, Montreal, Canada, October 1976.

8. Dodson, Betty. "Confessions of a Pleasure Junkie." *Forum*, June 1978.

9. Dodson, Betty. *Sex for One: The Joy of Selfloving*. New York: Harmony Books, 1987.

10. *Federal Register*, February 26, 1980.

11. Ladas, Alice, Beverly Whipple and John D. Perry. *The G Spot and Other Recent Discoveries about Human Sexuality*. New York: Dell, 1982.

12. Maines, Rachel. "Socially Camouflaged Technologies: The Case of the Electromechanical Vibrator." *Technology*, June 1989.

13. Maines, Rachel. "The Vibrator and Its Predecessor Technologies," presented at the Four Society Meeting, Pittsburgh, Pennsylvania, October 1986 (Society for the History of Technology, History of Science Society, Philosophy of Science Association, Society for the Social Study of Science).

14. Masters, William H. and Virginia E. Johnson. *Human Sexual Response*. Boston: Little, Brown, 1966.

15. Morin, Jack, Ph.D. *Anal Pleasure & Health*. Burlingame, CA: Yes Press, 1981, 1986.

16. Safran, Claire. "Plain Talk about the New Approach to Sexual Pleasure." *Redbook*, March 1976.

17. Sherfey, Mary Jane (quoted in Brecher, *The Sex Researchers*).

18. Swartz, Mimi. "For the Woman who has Almost Everything." *Esquire*, July 1980.

19. Wheeler, Connie and Tex Williams. "Vibrators: A His and Hers Guide." *Forum*, December 1975.

20. Whipple, Beverly and Gina Odgen. *Safe Encounters: How Women Can Say Yes to Pleasure and No to Unsafe Sex*. New York: McGraw-Hill, 1989.

21. Woods, Margo. *Masturbation, Tantra and Self Love*. San Diego: Omphaloskepsis Press (c/o Mho and Mho Works, Box 33135, San Diego CA 92103), 1981.

22. Zilbergeld, Bernie and Michael Evans. "Inadequacy of Masters and Johnson." *Psychology Today*, August 1980.

23. Zilbergeld, Bernie. *Male Sexuality*. New York: Bantam, 1979.

Joani Blank, MA, MPH

Joani Blank worked as a sex therapist and sex educator in the early 1970s. She taught human sexuality at the community college level, led sexuality workshops for women, was an active volunteer and trainer at San Francisco Sex Information and led therapy groups for pre-orgasmic women.

In the spring of 1975 she started DOWN THERE PRESS with the publication of *The Playbook for Women About Sex*. Down There Press now publishes the work of other authors as well as Joani's, and boasts a list of twelve titles.

In 1977 Joani published the first edition of *Good Vibrations*. She opened her retail store, also called Good Vibrations, the same year so that women would have a comfortable and non-threatening environment in which to learn about and buy vibrators and other sex toys.

The store and the subsequent growth of mail order sales also provided an outlet for her books. In 1988 Joani began a mail-order catalog of sex awareness and enhancement books called The Sexuality Library. She operated her companies democratically, and in 1992 sold the business to her employees, becoming an equal owner with them in a 100% worker-owned cooperative.

Joani is a graduate of Oberlin College and received her Master in Public Health degree from the University of North Carolina. She is active in the Society for the Scientific Study of Sex, and is a licensed Marriage, Family and Child Counselor.

For Vibrators by Mail

Good Vibrations
938-DT Howard Street, San Francisco CA 94103

Many of the vibrators, sex toys, and other items available at the store at 1210 Valencia Street. If you can't get to San Francisco, order this catalog! $2.00.

Eve's Garden
119 W. 57th Street, #420, New York NY 10019

A collection of "pleasurable things for women." $3.00.

My Choice
4951-D Clairemont Sq., #164, San Diego CA 92117

Some vibrators and a large selection of condoms. $3.00.

The Xandria Collection
P.O. Box 319005, San Francisco CA 94131

An assortment of adult products presented in an attractive format. $4.00 with signed statement that purchaser is over 21 years of age.

Voyages
P.O. Box 78550, San Francisco CA 94107-8550

Lotions, creams, vibrators, sex toys, books, videos and leather products. Free upon request, or $5.00 for a 6-catalog subscription.

Uniquity
P.O. Box 10, Galt CA 95632

Resources for mental health, including human sexuality. Offers vibrator accessories and books. FREE.

More Books from DOWN THERE PRESS/YES PRESS

_____ **Good Vibrations: The Complete Guide to Vibrators,** $5.50
Joani Blank.

_____ **Exhibitionism for the Shy,** *Carol Queen.* Show off, dress $12.50
up and talk hot. Available Spring 1995.

_____ **Femalia,** *Joani Blank, editor.* Thirty-two stunning color $14.50
photographs of vulvas by four photographers, for
aesthetic enjoyment and edification.

_____ **Herotica: A Collection of Women's Erotic Fiction,** $8.50
Susie Bright, editor. "...explores the outer boundaries
of erotica." *Lambda Rising Book Report*

_____ **Sex Information, May I Help You?,** *Isadora Alman.* $9.50
"...Difficult material handled well. An excellent
model on how to speak directly about sex." *San
Francisco Chronicle*

_____ **Erotic by Nature,** *David Steinberg, editor.* A luscious $42.50
volume of photos, line drawings, prose and poetry
for, by and of women and men. Clothbound.

_____ **The Playbook for Women About Sex,** *Joani Blank.* $4.50
Activities to enhance sexual self-awareness.

_____ **Anal Pleasure & Health,** *Jack Morin, Ph.D.* $12.50
Comprehensive guidelines for AIDS risk reduction.

_____ **Men Loving Themselves,** *Jack Morin, Ph.D.* $15.00
A beautiful photostudy of male masturbation.

_____ **The Playbook for Men About Sex,** *Joani Blank.* $4.50
Explores communication, sexual self-image.

Catalogs — free with purchase of any book

_____ **Good Vibrations Mail Order.** Many of the wonderful
items available in the San Francisco vibrator   store.

_____ **The Sexuality Library.** A mail order catalog with over
300 informative and entertaining sexual self-help and
enhancement books and videos.

Buy these books from your local bookstore, or use this coupon:

Down There Press, 938 Howard St., San Francisco CA 94103

Include $3.75 for orders up to $20.00. California residents please add
sales tax. We ship UPS whenever possible; please give us your street
address

Name_____

UPS Street Address_____

_____ ZIP_____